Out of the Ashes

Antoinette Peppler

Out of the Ashes
Copyright © 2019 Antoinette Peppler
LinkBookLegacies.com publishing
San Diego, California
All rights reserved.

Cover, layout and Design: Amy Sayer and Jon Sayer (www.eighty3five.co.uk)
Editor: Susan Fisher

ISBN # 978-0-359-98394-0

Printed in the United States of America.

To my mom.

Your love and encouragement gave me the strength to become the woman I am today. Thank you for always inspiring me to follow my heart and live my dreams. Dance with the angels mom, till we meet again, I will love you forever.

Contents

MISS VIOLA GRAND

---

*T*he first time we went to see our broken-down home was not only devastating, but debilitating. How can one explain all the feelings of loss, despair & sadness? You really can't unless you experience it. The words don't even express the magnitude of emotions one feels or can't feel. I'll never forget seeing my baby grand piano laying in the ashes. I had nick-named her Miss Viola, after her makers brand name, Viola Grand. I had purchased her only a few years before, after praying for a miracle to purchase a used baby grand. It was a dream come true when I had found her, at a price I could easily afford! I could barely see her ivory & ebony keys, or the top of her worn wooden lid that resonated such wondrous sounds. She had been tucked away in an elderly woman's mobile home, buried under books & clutter. I often wondered what magical hands had played her through the years. At 101 years old, she had lived through the roaring 20's, big band 30's & delta blues 40's. Strolling into the sock-hop 50's, she saw the birth of rock & roll in the 60's & 70's. She had seen it all! But today as I stared at my beauty Miss Viola, her glory was gone, her days of sweet music were ended. She had fallen from the top of the stairs down thru the floor and landed onto the hard garage floor. What was once my sweet Baby grand, was now nothing more than a rusted ole' cast iron sound board. Just metal strings & pins dangling, like twisted barbs of wire. Oh, how can this be? Is this what life can be reduced to? What once played music to my ears is now nothing but pieces of iron rods & worthless scraps of metal & ash. I could not contain my emotion as the tears filled my eyes & the grief stole my heart. How do I mend this brokenness? Why do I feel like this is who I am... a reflection of myself? I could still feel the fire when I touched her burnt metal plate, as my tears rolled down her board & fell to the ground. Oh, my heart... such sadness does despair! I cannot bear this thought as I see myself in there. Finally, here the song does rest, as I see the end of this beautiful story. As our lives are molded, shaped & played, the hand of the Father is never far away. He is near to the weary & broken-hearted, close to the hurting & downtrodden. If He cares for the lilies of the fields & the birds of the air, how much more valuable are we to our God! I keep Viola's memory alive, she's worth much more to me than gold. Perhaps that's what I'm meant to say, He loves us more than we will ever know!

10 FINGERS & TOES

I remember the small things. Those fun times planning big events & birthday celebrations. Sitting around the table at holiday meals with family, loved ones & friends. Baseball games, football teams & wrestling matches. Trophy awards, prom nights, graduation, college education & wedding bell bliss. Laughing, crying, singing the blues & praising the Lord! All those memories we held dear to our hearts, because they were with the ones we love. I hold on to these thoughts now, they are more precious to me every day. I try not to forget. All those things we made, created & bought expressed who we are & what we were. Yet they seem to grow less & less important when I think about what really matters most. Like the first kiss from my sweetheart & the first time I counted my lil' boys' fingers & toes. The bond we share with those we love & the moments we make in life are timeless... ageless & unforgettable. Those emotions we feel, when we envision those special pictures in time, capture our thoughts & steal our hearts. That's what matter most now. We can still remember yesterday. We are alive today to tell our story & share our lives into tomorrow. I will keep this loss, rather than endure the loss of my loved ones. That's what I have learned to be thankful for, I can still count those 10 fingers & toes.

13TH OF SEPTEMBER

A letter to my sons:

I know you're heartbroken, devastated & dismayed right now. I feel your pain & know what you're going through. I wish I could kiss it away & make it all better. That's a mother's love... to only want the best for her children. You don't understand, you want to go back to how it was before, but you can't. You keep asking, "why?". You were starting a new life, settling in & enjoying where you were. I've been there. I know how you feel; I've felt this same way too. It was only just 2 years ago when we lost our home to a fire, but it feels like yesterday. All of you came to our side, held us up with your love & support after we lost everything. But now, those all familiar feelings have started all over again, but this time they are for you. I can tell you, it will not always be like this. This too shall pass, it will get better. Look at what you have come thru & where you are today. You have suffered a great loss, something so many are experiencing as well. You're not alone! God carried us thru & I know He will carry you too. September 13th was the beginning of a new life for us; the day your Dad & I married. We raised you boys with a love & determination, so you could make the most of everything in life. You CAN do all things through Christ who gives you strength! So be strong my sons, YOU are our legacy, remember you are never alone! I love you more than you will ever know... Mom 💔

15 STEPS FROM FIRE

---

*W*hen the fire took our home, it changed our lives & things have never been the same. I had to accept that from the very beginning. The sooner I did, the sooner I could move on. This was not the end of my life; this was just another chapter in my journey. I had to turn the page. But I will never forget that day. How can I? It was a hot & windy Labor Day. We were unwinding & relaxing after a long holiday weekend. Our home was cooled & the blinds were drawn shut, to keep out the blazing heat of the sun. We were completely unaware of the raging fire that was around us. Had our son Jimmy not come home to check on us, I would not be telling this part of the story. Even though the fire had breached our property, he continued down the long narrow road, keeping watch at the flames approaching our home. He quickly drove up to the house & frantically called for his Dad & I. When I looked up, I saw 2 pillars of flames rolling down the hillside. It was ripping & roaring like waves of flames, crashing & pounding on the hillside! The sight & sound was frightening & it was headed for our home. Little did I realize that the picture Jimmy painted for us the Christmas before, would be so prophetic & symbolic to our story. Like the Lord covering us under the shadow of His wings, parting the fire that approached us... we were safe. When Jimmy yelled downstairs... "Mom? There's a fire!!!!".
It took me 15 steps to climb those stairs, to face the fire that would change my life forever! 🔥

STANDING AT MY POST

*T*oday has been a somber day. I watched the funeral service for our nation's 41st President, George H.W. Bush. At the same time, I stood watching from our studio window, as many of you drove up Pentz road to see the remains of your homes. Two different processions, one same purpose. To put to rest a life. One for our nation & one for the homes of many of you. My heart goes out to each of you. Though this is most difficult, it is necessary that we have closure to our loss. It's important to see the remains of your home. Take a breath. You're not alone. As you take this drive to destination home, I stand with you as a nation, a town & one heart that mourns the loss of so many. Your homes & businesses are what built the foundation of Paradise. A solemn day, a mournful time for our town. Let us stand together as we take a knee, say a prayer & like the Phoenix, we shall rise again out of the ashes!

18

17 TREASURES MORE

A picture says a thousand words. I'm digging through ashes & shattered glass of a broken-down home. Who would have thought that one could ever find anything worth saving? Just take a lil' piece of my heart again & again & again. A treasure box of remnants & charred burnt jewelry. A rusted silver baby spoon, a handle less spatula & many broken ceramic pots. Handcrafted suns, moons, plus melted pots & pans. Oh my heart... deep down, my soul just ached, as I felt the sorrow drop me to my knees. My cheeks were covered with black soot, my clothes had the smell of smoke. I brushed the hair from my eyes with my glove covered hand and wiped the tears from my face. "Don't stop" I said. "Keep digging!" Perhaps I'll find something, anything that I could hold on to & say... this made it! And then I realized, all these broken pieces were broken treasures from my life that once was. I keep them as a reminder that though these things look worthless to many, they are priceless to me. They are my broken treasures from my broken life. They're reminders of my life before. 17 treasures & more. 💔

20 TEARS FROM HEAVEN

One by one the raindrops fell as we drove through town today. Tree after tree was burnt, blackened, fallen to the ground, cut & stacked. Our stops were few but memorable. My sons' house had stucco laid flat to the ground, where ashes covered what was once his home. I could feel my sons' sadness as he stared in disbelief that this was now his life. All he had left was what he'd left town with. Everything else was gone... all of it! We left with a heavy heart as he said his goodbyes to his home. Through the maze of workers, shadows of brick houses & black & gray covered streets, we stopped at our other sons' place. We all were somber, staring at the remnants of what was left of a broken-down home. We walked around & recognized several pieces & things that once were whole. Out of the bottom of the ash covered floor, lay a face staring back at me. I lifted it up, brushed it off & recognized the statue of Saint Francis of Assisi. Out of the ashes comes Beauty! A memory for my son to remember that he is still alive! A memory for all of us, that though our sorrow is great, our prayers have been heard. 20 more tears from heaven rained down on me today, tears for sadness & tears of joy. Though my sons' homes are gone, just like ours was, they too shall rise from the ashes. Be strong my sons, you are our legacy... a part of God's history! 💔

21 JUMP STREET

---

*H*ard to return to "normal" when nothing is normal at all. Kinda feels like trying to fit into last year's jeans, the ones that are 2 sizes too small! Gets over the rear but ya just can't zip it up... nothing fits! It all feels like everything is outta place. Keep doing the same thing over & over. That plant over there needs to go in the corner. No, maybe by the TV... oh wait... that's right, I don't have a TV! All those memories of what's lost is magnified at the holidays. Maybe it's because everything you want to buy for someone else doesn't make sense when you need to buy it for yourself. Gotta put on a happy face, a smile so no one sees my pain. Can't move, my mind's racing a mile a minute, or not at all. If I pretend that everything's alright then maybe, just maybe, I can feel something. Playing undercover cop in a made-up world that doesn't exist anymore. Like 21 Jump Street. An undercover cop going back to High School to play a student but, he's really a cop playing the person that he never was, in a class that he doesn't belong in. It's kinda like that... I think... I don't know anymore! Maybe I'll just put on my wonder woman mask & be somebody else today. Ah dang it, she doesn't wear a mask!?!? 🤦

CHANGES...

Really!? Wow, how can a person deal with all the changes that happen in an instant, a moment, a life changing event in time? Boy, one thing for sure, when tragedy strikes you really see who your family & friends really are. Right?! Sometimes the generosity & love from strangers is even more heartfelt. That's okay, I'll take it, anytime! When ya feel like your world is falling apart, because it is, the last thing you need is judgment & criticism. If I've been misunderstood, talk to me instead of everybody else. If I've miscommunicated my intentions, let me show you who I really am! "Ch ch ch ch changes..." as the writer sings, defies his critics while he steps out on his own. "Time may change me, but I can't trace time". It's time to step ahead, out of the comfort zone & defy the odds. Perhaps this change is not just to our homes & town. Maybe the change is letting go, not just of what we've lost, but of those who've tried to bring us loss, misery & harm. I'm moving on, letting go of the past. I'm making a change to better my world, with those who see the value of working together, instead of working against each other. I believe in a better tomorrow! I've seen beauty for ashes when my sorrow turned to joy, after I felt Gods presence. I'm not perfect & never have been... but He is! 🌹

24 HOURS A DAY...

I'm missing Paradise! All the people, friends & loved ones. The familiar places, spaces & faces. We lived in a town surrounded by such glorious & magnificent God given beauty! Now it's almost unbearable to drive through town. Because I know every time I do, it will be something different than it was on the day before yesterday. How do we replace this heartache with happiness? When do we start feeling that peace that passes all understanding? Our lives will never be the same! I've seen the look in your eyes, the sadness in your smile & the pain in your heart. We're all trying to move on, but we're feeling the loss that we all have lost. It don't come easy, nothing ever does & this my friend is no exception. All those things we'd wished to be different. If only I can, but I can't & that's a fact. We can't go back to what was, but we can go on to what is. No, it's not the same & it never will be, but we can make a difference in making it better. We're starting over again & I'm trying to be okay with that. I'm trying to keep my eyes on the One who's got the whole world in His hands. When I give it to Him, I no longer have my world on my shoulders, but I have His peace in my heart. I know then, that I will be alright. I can, I will, I'm able, because God is able to work all things for good. I'm holding on to that now... 24 hours a day. ☀

27

25 CENTS

---

*H*ave you noticed? Nothing seems to make sense lately. The devastation is unbelievably overwhelming! This disaster has not only changed our life, but everyone else's too. All those feelings of uneasiness, along with an underlying sense of anxiousness & nervousness, is constant. It's almost like a feeling of being lost, with a dash of numbness & a drop of depression. Where do I go from here? I didn't question so much before & now I question myself & everything else. Even if I'm not in town, even if I get away from it all, my heart is still broken wherever I go. Gotta give ourselves a break... really! I'm not okay, I guess that's okay. I know I'm being real, perhaps too real with what I feel & how I share. It's all a growth process, baby steps, taking one day, one moment at a time. Things can & do change, even if I make a plan ahead of time! If you could say one thing to someone else to help, what would that be? Here's mine: my 25-cent advice...
K I S S, keep it simple sweetheart!

26 ANGELS

*A*s I passed the burnt & scorched fields along 99 to Durham Pentz Rd., I came to the sight of blackened trees & burned down homes. I stopped & gazed upon the darkened landscape that now lined the charred terrain. There were widow trees & brush that still defaced the surrounding hills, from the 2016 Saddle Fire, that destroyed our previous home. We had just rebuilt & moved in, celebrating being home again, before the Camp Fire hit. It changed our lives & nothing has been the same. As I returned on this Thanksgiving Day, I looked around in dismay & wondered at what I saw. For 360' around our home & property, there were new remnants & evidence of the Camp Fire that surrounded us. But it did not touch us! It's as if Heaven's Army of Angels encamped around us & sheltered us under their wings. I could not hold back the tears as I realized what I saw. This was a miracle before my very eyes! I don't deserve this gift, but I'm so very grateful to God for it! Though we were protected this time from the flames, it has left a scar upon our hearts & souls. We feel it, but this we know, we are alive because God's grace still abounds. He is our shelter & I am trusting in Him! "But You are a tower of refuge to the poor, O Lord, a tower of refuge to the needy in distress. You are a refuge from the storm & a shelter from the heat".

26 Angels & more....

Isaiah 25:4

THINGS TO PONDER

———————

reaming, thinking, waiting during sleepless nights, restless mornings & wasted days. I see the painted sunset as the bright lit moon appears in the darkened nite sky. Try to sit down, relax & turn on a movie, but I'm already watching one playing in my head! Anxious thoughts & stressful clutter fill my mind throughout the hazy day. Gotta focus, have much to do, but can't move. Makin a list, checkin it twice, my energy has now been all but used up. Really! Try to sleep, so fatigued & tired, but I keep seeing sugar plums dancing in my head?! Wait... what?! Where did that come from? Trauma, drama, anxiety & stress, call it what ya want, it zaps the strength right out of the super men & women that we are. Gotta look at the beauty, not the ashes. See that precious lil' fractured treasure? I found it delicately broken, laying on the burnt ground. Yet when I look at it pieced together again; I see hope... if only for a moment. That gift I was given by a stranger, gives me joy for this mourning & grief. Oh... that colorful sweater my sweet friend just gave me; this's my garment of praise & thanksgiving for a new day. These are the things I must fix my thoughts on right now; that which is true, honorable & right. That which is lovely & admirable. I must think about things that are excellent & worthy of praise & thanksgiving. Because I can choose to rejoice in the things that are before me; family & friends, nature & music, love & all that is good in life. Yet what will sustain me when I ponder this thought, is less of what I can see & more of what I can't. It's in faith that I believe that God gives me strength; He carry's me, holds me & brings me thru it. This is my assurance, my hope, the reality I know... that God has not finished in me, the work He began!

Philippians 4:8

33

TIME FOR PEACE

$\mathcal{A}$s I open my journal, pen in my hand, coffee cup in the other, I'm ready to conquer the day. It's time! Time to start fighting back this deep sadness that keeps trying to steal my joy. As I put the pen to the paper, I'm holding back tears. I push through a flood of emotions to let the ink tell my story. I'm searching for peace to calm this storm of despair. So much to tell, as my hand races to keep up with the thoughts in my head. The work has begun, a new page has been turned in a new chapter of my life. I'm ending this battle that has wearied & captured my soul. I'm leaving it here on these pages. I'll no longer carry this burden, this weight. I'm tired & worn but I won't lose this fight! I put on my armor, my sword in my hand. There is no defeat, there's only an end. An end to this hopeless, pitiful sorrow & dismay. So, I'm cutting the cord & here it shall lay, on this tear stained page, here it shall stay. "For everything there is a season, a time for every purpose under heaven. A time to weep & a time to laugh. A time to grieve & a time to dance. A time to tear down & a time to build up. A time to love & a time to hate. A time for war & a time for peace." I have won this battle today, put an end to this war!
It is now time for Peace & time to restore.

Ecc.3:1,4,7,8.

WIDOW MAKER

---

*O*ur home's founding landmark has finally fallen. She was once that one resilient tree that represented so much hope to our shattered world. But after 2 years of watching her oak green leaves fade, her broken limbs & brittle bark break, she had become a danger to our home. She was indeed the grandest of them all. Now, she had become just another "widow maker" tree. As I watched her slowly fall, I shed a tear & said a prayer. I was thankful to have had such a stoic reminder to never give up in the face of danger. Her tenacity to endure the heat of the fire, that stole our 1st home; gave her such grace & beauty for me to hope in a better tomorrow. She was a symbol to us, a beacon in the storm, a tower of strength, that shaded our weary souls. As I pass the fallen landmarks of our town, I'm also reminded of all the precious times I found hope, in a place I called home. It's a bittersweet moment to watch this huge change unfold before us. But then I remember that pillar of hope that stood strong. Like a light house through the storm, at once I'm able to make peace with the past. I'm able to accept all those things that I know I cannot change. My "widow maker" landmark is now put to rest. In her place, we'll plant another landmark tree for our home. A living legacy that brings honor, strength & dignity, to represent the town that we are proud of. Paradise Strong!!!

HEART STRINGS

---

*H*ard to let go when ya can't think straight. Sometimes it feels like another lifetime, a different world, an unspoken dream. The mind does not always register the difference between time & space, because our heart holds onto the cords that bind our love for home. It's the memories that keep reminding us of another place where we found security, rest & a buffered refuge from the storms of this life.

So how do we let go of this longing desire, to fill this need? Our empty nest, this broken heart. It's not just loss, this is death. We couldn't move on completely until we accepted that. So, we had a memorial service for our home, just the two of us. We each wrote a letter to our home, from the memories, love, heartache & loss. We prayed, we cried & we held each other as we tossed our letters into one of the only things that survived... our fire pit. We said our goodbyes as we watched the flames take the words from the page & the smoke filled the air with our prayers towards heaven. Finally, we felt a release. We were free to move on from those ties that held our hearts & constantly tortured our souls. It was time to rise out of the ashes & begin something new. It was time to mend & time to end, time to let go of those things I called heartstrings.

40

CASTLES IN THE SAND

---

*J*ust when I felt I could take a deep breath, my heart started to break... I'd fallen again! I can still hear their words like an echo in my head. From a distant hushed murmur, to a shout from within. How could they not know, I'd heard what they said? How could they not see from their faces, I read! They pointed a finger & slowly I bled, from their two-edged sword that cut deep to my soul. So fragile I was & vulnerable too, but if tender I was, then I easily bruised. I tried to explain how my life had just changed, but I tired of telling my story again. Like my crumbled down castle lay spread in the sand, it felt like my heart had been crushed once again. I thought to myself; "No you don't understand, I'm not finished yet. I've only begun something new in the sand!" I'm not over this, I know I'm not done, but give me this moment, I'm broken again. I don't need a judge, I need only a friend. One right beside me to lend me a hand & one who'll be there to help me defend. I may have lost much but my dignity stands, so come let us reason & make castles in the sand.

41

SHADOW OF WINGS

Sometimes I think or don't think, maybe I just can't think. I'm going through the motions of what I need to do, don't wanna do, probably can't do. It still gets me, or I don't get it, still can't get ahold of my new reality. I just don't feel it somedays, like I'm looking out of a stained-glass window, but the colors all seem gray. "I can't give up!" I say to myself. Deep down inside I feel like it all seems meaningless. A season of mourning through the cloudy days, brings shadows of changes that I don't want to admit, I don't want to accept. Yet then I see it, a ray of sunlight breaks through that iridescent glass & I feel the warmth on a cold winter day. Then right before my weary eyes, a red tailed, golden speckled hawk, spreads its magnificent wings. It tilts to wave a grandstand greeting! I gasp for breath as I'm moved by such a display of incredible beauty. In an instant... for just a precious moment, my strength is renewed. My hope is restored & I accept this sign as a gift from God. I can't change the outcome of what has been, but I can change my perspective of what will be. I want to see the everyday blessings before me, because these will bring hope & purpose through these disconnected days. A beautiful sunrise that wakes my morning day, as I watch the simple pleasures of life unfold through nature, music, a smile from a stranger, or a kiss from a loved one. This I know! I can... more than that, I need to abide, under the shadow of His wings. This is where I will find shelter & rest through these restless troubled times.

1ST LOVE

---

*T*hey say you never forget your first love. That first kiss, like an impressionable moment that exists in time immemorial. I'd have to say, I definitely agree. We tend to remember those tender moments & awestruck feelings of emotion, that captured our hearts & deepened our souls. This is how I felt about Paradise. That first time I discovered our quaint little town. What was it that stole our hearts & planted our feet into solid ground? We finally could gratefully say, "we are home"! Was it the tall Digger Pines with the sharp pointed cones, or the scrubby green Oakes? How they nestled the noisy blue jays & fed those busy bodied squirrels! Maybe it was those grand black Oakes, where Rocky Raccoon & his bandito brothers played. Chasing up & down the trees, we spotted their beady bright eyes, hiding behind the thick crackled bark. Bambi would visit with her spotted friend Thumper & eat all those new blossomed roses, that sprung us into the new season of Spring. Daffodils, lilies, lilacs and more, graced their beauty over the hillside & lined the creeks & riverbed shores. We danced through the night sipping wine under the light of the Summer moon; listening to the sound of a cooing dove or distant hooting of a wise ole' owl. Who could not fall in love with those hot endless days, as we swam in the sun warmed lake? We walked down the jagged path by the waters that flowed through the old miner's flume. It was like heaven.... the newness, the discovery of a hidden treasure that held our hearts & kept us whole. But just like first love, it changes. Unfolding, reshaping & recreating into something less glorious, that seems more like a chore. Aw... at last we've come to the crossroads. We dare to push ourselves in the challenge to dig deep to our core & gather the strength to be more than a conqueror, a warrior at best! Our quest lies ahead to finish this race, where we shall replant, remake & recreate. Our journey is long, our destiny hard, a fight to remember what we once had begun. When we ran we worked, we strived to hold on to what we had captured, though perhaps it was not what we captured, but what captured us. It simply was this; our hearts had been smitten like that moment in time, with a kiss we had risen. We thought we'd found it, but now we finally know; what happened was not that we found it, but it had found us. 1st love!

MR. POTTER SMITH

I've turned this page, intrigued to know more, I read as His story unfolds: Mr. Smith takes the silver, though cold to the touch, he hammers the metal, till it bends & it folds. He knows as he works it, it hardens & molds, by the force of his hand, he can shape a new stand. But careful he is, not to quicken the blow, for he must use the heat, to soften the load. He's careful & sure, with the flame to apply, or the metal will crack & break from the cold. The next day, Mr. Smith uses his raw & pure gold. Though it's supple & soft, combined with the heat, the silver & gold, he yields a new piece. He creates something colorful, stronger & true, from out of the ashes, comes a beautiful hue. Potter now takes his place at the wheel. He gathers his clay & adds water to feel, the shape of his work, though fragile...it's real! To perfect his creation by sealing the clay, he fires the pot at a lower temp blaze. He then cools the vase, paints a colorful glaze, then fires this beauty under flame once again. He places his artwork, so much to behold, on the stand he'd created from silver & gold. He looks at his work, how alike is his life; his struggles seemed hard, as his heart had been hurt. Now weary & worn, weak & afraid, he warms himself carefully by the heat of the kiln. He slowly is softened by the words of his friend, "take courage, be strong, together we can!" He thinks to himself, "who am I, just a man?". But just like the clay, though once only a lump, had become something much more than he'd ever hoped for. The fire had shaped, molded & sealed, what he had made & formed on the wheel. It's not what we were, not just what we are, but what we will be, what we're to become. He thinks to himself, the trials of this life, though wearing & hard, shall never define us. They never shall make us, but simply said, they are here to refine us. I put down the book, left a marker in place, I pondered then whispered, "I thank you for this, Mr. Potter Smith".

SAMSON & DELILAH

... are the names I have given to our two beautiful & majestic osprey hawks. I often see them circling high above the pale blue skies, catching the updraft of a wind as they fly around our burnt & tattered property. Like royalty, they confidently perch on the branch of a blackened & broken Digger Pine. They're gazing out at the dark terrain. I've watched them grow since they first left the safety & comfort of their aerie home, a bulky stick piled nest. I've often wondered what they must see, perhaps what they might think, as they're looking down at me & I'm staring back motionless, looking up at them. Do they remember how it was before, as they wander out upon the charred remains? When they soared above the green forest & searched below the bay leaf shrubs & the sage brush floor, for their challenged hunt. Do they remember how they played with the wild untamed creatures of the nite & danced with the gallant sprite gypsies of the day, lurking to find that perfect prey? I watched & waited anxiously, to see their long return. They too had left their homes from the terrorizing flames & ashen smoke, that burned & filled the thick black air. There was no sign of my predator friends, no distant cry that screeched the sky until the time was right & they graced our presence once again. I saw them brush the crisp cool air with their feathered wings, that seemed to touch each other. Their voices sang that joyful scream! I'm blessed to be amongst such magnificent beauty. To see their strength, endurance, long suffering, companionship & perseverance. It's an encouragement to me, to never give up! When I see them, my hope is restored & my faith is renewed. My spirit is lifted up & my heart becomes full. I'm grateful to see such incredible & awesome beauty, that has risen from the ashes! Samson & Delilah came home again today, perhaps it was not just for me, but maybe it was for you too. Don't ever give up my friends, we can rise above the ashes too & begin again something new!

OUR TOWN

*W*hat can I say? Thank you! Thank you for allowing me into your world & letting me share a part of mine. I am deeply touched by the overwhelming response that each one of you has graciously expressed, through sharing your precious stories with me. It gives me such a light of hope & encouragement, to know that I am not alone in this struggle. We are not alone in this battle, we are in this fight together. Our memorable town, our remarkable lives, have desperately reached the point of no return. No going back, we have boldly stood & stated a NO to defeat! We have started the difficult process of back breaking clearing, tedious cleaning & unending debris removal. It's not very pretty, just heartbreaking to watch, our downtrodden town constantly changing on a daily basis. Everyday, as I cautiously drive through the many vacant lots, down the darkened tattered streets, I sense the void of emptiness. I feel the stabbing pains of labor as we go through this transitional stage of rebuilding. I know this all too well. I have been living it as I grieve for each one of you, because I know it's not only my loss, it's not just your loss, but it's our loss. It's not easy to watch the center of our lives, the heart of our homes & all that we once had, be carefully fallen. So scrupulously scraped & everything reduced & compressed, to be tactfully hauled off to nowhere land. It hurts to see all we've worked for & owned, all our creative hard work, reduced to disfigured metal. Just crushed glass & molten ash. But it's not the end, simply the beginning of a beautiful mess, that will clear the way for a better & brighter tomorrow. It will prepare the freshly filled ground, to lay the building foundation for a new home, a new life, a new town. When I see all the hard hat workers, sign yielding street stoppers & cleat shod tree climbers; I try to hold back the tears as I crack a smile, wave & say, "thank you for your service". My mind is silently screaming, my heart is constantly breaking, but somehow deep inside... a voice keeps saying; "Be strong & courageous, you are not alone". I might be slightly broken, we may be quietly hurting, but that's okay. We'll be alright because we're all doing this together, for a better cause & the greater good of tomorrow. I'm leaving a light on, for "Our Town".

TOMBSTONE CHIMNEY

*A*s I struggled with my wandering thoughts, I finally reached a different conclusion. After much deliberation, what seemed to make no sense, made perfect sense to me! I know this must sound odd, but this is what I've found. Somehow it doesn't feel like this is real to me. Quite honestly, I don't see how it possibly can be. When I take that somber drive throughout our fallen town, it definitely becomes surreal, in a closer distant way. It's like that classic western when the rancher's family gasp & weep, as they stare in disbelief. A devastating calamity, much to their dismay, their homestead, land, their life, seemed completely wiped away. In a moment, an instant, all they had is lost. What is left just stands alone, their bedrock tombstone chimney! This witness to their purpose, their life it represents; a landmark souvenir, a tower in the dark. Their lonely desperation, this all familiar scene; I'm watching from the outside but, I'm seeing from within. It hits a chord that grieves my heart yet binds me closer to; connecting to my neighbors, new friends & family. What happens next, I must confess, seems quite remarkable. This next scene is the beauty of why we can't forget. The hardship of the lone prairie life shared the trail with these pioneers. Now these same ones came to help, to comfort & rebuild. This family's towered bedrock, their lonesome chimney stack, no longer just a grave site marker, to display their shattered past. But now much more it has become, a special place, a cornerstone, to their present future cast. That's the true grit reality I want to focus on. Not the one of disbelief but this, community. Side by side, step by step, I've seen the hands of mercy. The gentle arms of love amongst our bravest townspeople, through this loss they rise above. Now I see these landmarks as I drive down crooked lanes, or up the hillside patchy roads, around to center streets. They're a haunting memorial, of what our precious lives once stood for. Yet what they are today, is not what they shall stay, but what they shall become. I look upon these talking towers as monuments my friend, not just red brick chimney stacks. For now, they tell a different story. A new scene will begin in the bedrock of our home, our town, our memorable Tombstone Chimneys!

HOPE REBORN

Thinking, dreaming, looking out through the hazy mist of what lies ahead. This long journey has been challenging! A difficult fighting battle to survive, as we walk through the remains of what the fire has left. Ashes of grief. It's a constant underlying struggle to conquer these lonely, lost feelings. Depression tries to capture our wandering thoughts, our indecisive minds & our hurting hearts. Our perfect little world has drastically changed. This unique journey we're traveling on, is often wearing, though it serves a purpose to our path. We're Survivors, Sojourners, Pioneers, on a pilgrimage to a different & rediscovered land. We're in uncharted territory! When I'm walking through the valley of the shadow of sadness, I must remind myself to put one feeble foot in front of the other. I'm trying to be valiantly strong, through this great & terrible loss. It's part of the process. The good, the bad, the ugly days & wasted nights, conflict our scattered thoughts. In the end, they deepen our inner growth. I must keep turning the ever-changing page, reading a new & different chapter. These tiresome days are surely numbered & this fleeting moment will soon pass. What appears now shall not always be, in this season of our lives. The cold winter nights give birth to a new life in the warm spring days. Yesterday is forever gone, today has faithfully come, but tomorrow is a new day. We are on an adventurous quest, a destined journey, to a hope reborn from the ashes! We shall begin anew as we continue to venture on this journey, if only one step, one moment, one day at a time.

TOMORROW'S DREAM

*L*ike a lost memory in pieces of scattered time, I overlook the cloudy shadow of an unforgotten place I once lived. Constant & changing, moving in the bitter wind like a gentle whisper or a silent roar. I faintly remember the wonder filled times, when I felt so much alive. I was so quickly inspired to make my footprint in the ground, take my perfect spot & settle in this beautiful place called Paradise. If only I hadn't lost that precious moment, that living dream; the distant reality that became a nightmare in the dark. But now I anxiously wait, as I widely stare into my daydreamed thoughts & prepare for the dawn of a new day. Do I even dare, do I even try to dream again & rise quietly from my silent scream? I stagger about in my demise & despair. Is it here that I can really find what I am looking for? Can I still feel something deep inside that will stir my soul again? Can I be more than I am, at this moment in time? I've pondered this gracious gift that I've undeservingly been given & have chosen to take this imperfect path. I must take this bold risk & say yes to this newfound hope, this rescue plan, to see through yesterday's sorrow into the birth of a new tomorrow. I'm no longer desperate & alone; I have so much to see & behold! Though I feel like I can't, I know I can be more than I am. My eyes have seen the glory, I have felt His Mighty hand! He can make this something beautiful again! Today I'm peering through a blurred windowpane, as I see my broken reflection staring back at me. Like a crackled spotty mirror, I can dimly peek thru this looking glass. Finally, I have seen it! This hope, that yearning, the vision I have, is for "Tomorrow's Dream"!

BEAUTY IN THE ASHES

It's this. The look I see, in this mesmerizing mural. It's especially daunting, yet an unmistakably stellar display of beauty & grace. I see so much depth in her, I feel like I must know her, maybe I have seen her. Perhaps, I have even met her. It's a stare of passionately knowing, a wistful smile that tenderly breaks, to show a sage-like wisdom. The smoky tone in her face & the sultry stance, delicately show her confidence. It gives way to an undeniable competence in her graceful demeanor. She proves to be a pillar of hope that lightens the burden of doubt. It's a feeling I get when I glance into her deepened eyes. I'm moved by her soft gentle smile, that captivates my transparent thoughts & makes me think all things are possible again! I'm captured by the presence of a beauty in the ashes, as I realize what once was lost, shall now be found. My tears have stained the ashen ground once more, yet they are drops of relief. I realize I am called out of this darkness & into His wonderful light! I'm delightfully amazed, perhaps quietly awakened, to see through these hazy days & open my eyes to a new morning.... a fresh start! Those piercing eyes have broken this hold, that binds my feet from moving forward. It's released the vicious snare that brings me down to deep despair. What seemed to be impossible, has now become possible; as I freely let go & boldly take hold of the One, who is greater than this. I am able to breathe, I am stronger to live! I am capable of dreaming again, because now I can see, Beauty in these Ashes.

REFLECTING

---

*T*here's something in the moving way she's standing still. As if bowing her head in reflective prayer, she's consciously drifting into a place where there is no other. Her long wispy hair, blowing in the cool night wind, is caught by a gentle breeze. It softly catches her breath. She wears a blissful smile, as she gathers her inner thoughts & deeply ponders the wonders of what could possibly be. Life does that, makes us reflect upon ourselves & examine our motives. It probes those aspirations, till we can firmly see a clear direction. Unanswered questions grasp a hold & take control of those random choices, simple tasks & man-made plans. The unmarked road is not always easy to know, which destined path is best to go. Sometimes we fly on a broken wing & silent prayer; unsure of what to do, where to go, or how we even got here! The simple answers to life's difficult struggles & unpredictable changes, are never found easily, without complete honesty & humble searching. It's time to stop, take a deep breath, cease the somber moment & sincerely reconnect. As we take a knee, let's say a heartfelt prayer to reach the gates of heaven & quietly listen, to the One who touches our wounded soul & heals our broken heart. The rest of the story has not finished, it has barely begun! Let us have ears to hear as we gain our bearings, cast our sorrows & learn to trust in this time of Reflecting.

JESUS

---

*L*ord, I'm tired. This is so exhausting. As I stand beside the honorable brave, I watch their humble efforts, trying to emulate their deeds & be more like them & less like me. But I am a wounded warrior from a futile fight, a fallen soldier in the dark! I don't know how much more weight, these shoulders can possibly bear, or muster up the strength. How can I gather the composure to battle the arrows that fly by day, when the aimless darts steal my restless sleep at night? I know I am only one amongst many, who feel this crippling weakness. This huge forbearance is an honest compulsion to want to be strong, but so quickly I become weak. I'm seeking refuge from this ruthless savage war. It took the helpless, our precious own; yet left so many to battle & wander on their own. Hear our prayer oh Lord! We need Your strength to endure the tempting trials, that befall the race ahead & cause this wavering doubt. Take this mustard seed of faith, though small it be, we ask for more. More faith to move forward, more strength to grow broader, more hope to believe that we are not alone! Help us know that You shall guide our crooked weary path. Heal our broken shattered hearts, to feel Your unfailing, everlasting love! Lord, please hold onto me, don't ever let me go; as I cling tightly to just a thread of hope. With You I know I'm strong, not weak. Open my eyes to see less of me & more of You, Jesus.

FACE OF THE FOREST

*I*f only the trees, the timber, the forest, had a voice that could speak. They would share from the deep of the woods. This is that face, although subtle, this stare tells the story of wishes, last rites, & bedside tales. She silently whispers an echo unheard, like a soft breezy wind that quickly returns. I quiver to think when I look at these trees, what a cry they might scream; "No! This can't be, look at me while I stand, before I have fallen from glory, before my beauty's no more"! They once were so vibrant & strong, embraced by the light, they stood spectacular, our gentle green giants. Such grace they displayed surrounding our town, giving us shade as they stood their ground. I gasp as I see this stunning lady, her speechless expression draws attention! She somberly captures a look of dismay, as she realizes the plight that befalls her bark timbers. It's a shock of disbelief, maybe a plea for a picture to remember her glory, our stately wood wonders. Now quiet & solemn they lay on the ground weeping in sorrow, our fallen grand arbors! Let us not soon forget how much beauty they brought to our humble abodes, to our quaint little town. This face of the forest speaks louder than words. I'm struck by the mystery of what I have heard. "Take a pinecone, an acorn, a sapling or seedling. Replant, restore, replace them once more"! In memory of what we once cherished & adored, let's bring back new growth to reshape our new town. Through the years they graced us with beauty & stature, let's honor these tree lives with bringing in new life. A silent request, perhaps a call from the wild, this from our lady, the Face of the Forest.

MISSY GRAMMER

"*Now* I lay me down to sleep, I pray the Lord my soul to keep..." a simple childhood bedside prayer. I remember the words so well. My Mama taught me to fold my hands, kneel by my bed & together we prayed. Seems a long time ago, those wonder filled days of yesteryear. Many four seasons have come & gone, but I'll never forget the sweet comfort she gave me, through the storms of this trying life. Isn't it funny how a picture reminds us of those little tucked memories in a box? They can say a thousand words without speaking a one! This is that memory, the picture I see as I look at sweet Missy, who peacefully sleeps through the cold of winters bitter past. That subtle tone beneath her crackled face, shows wear & tear from the heated flames & freezing snow. I can almost feel the stinging bite from the fire & ice, as I watch her still calmness without a care in the world. Sometimes I lay awake at night with my tired eyes wide open. I try so hard to stop the rambling thoughts of the day. I carefully check off my numbered list & try to forget what endless things were missed. The restless nights & daydreamed hours often fill this broken time with wandering thoughts & stressful talks. I think back on a moment in time, when my little boy's sleep would awaken. He'd cry with a fright & a scare, from a nightmare that seemed so real. I quietly prayed, softly combed through his hair & we'd cite a scripture to help calm his fear. "In peace I will lie down and sleep, for You alone Lord, make me dwell in safety". From a mother to a daughter, now a mother to a son, I continued a simple tradition. A prayer that led the babe-like child safe to the hands of the Father, was passed down & around & the circle was now complete. When anxious thoughts do multiply, I know where I can find a way to ease my stress, a comfort to settle my soul. A perfect reminder from this Mural I see, there is peace through the storm & a rest to our sleep. Through the heat of the fire & the freeze of the ice, Missy Grammer lays calm as she quietly sleeps.

Psalm 4:8

UNEXPECTED HOPE

I'm torn. The conflicting steps of moving onward, looking forward & planning ahead. Not seeing the many familiar faces, comfortable places, or green open spaces. Our impressionable minds continue to hold on to the memorable pictures we'd seen so many times before. Like walking down sweet memory lane & strolling through the echoes of our unforgotten life. Our tender hearts long for the precious memories & fond moments that touched our daily lives. I can't help it, I miss that. When I cautiously drive through our fallen down town, I grasp for the visual of what once stood on those empty spaces, now stacked with charred wood. I strive to remember our country bumpkin places, not the scraps of torn metal & chards of red brick. When it's least expected I'm pleasantly surprised, when I see an old face from the near distant past. Whether I know them or not, they're now a new friend, I'm glad to see someone I recognize again. It quiets the sadness of watching this process, that's clearing a way to making new progress. Though many have gone, have traveled afar, I know that their hearts still long for their home. Even those who have stayed probably question to go, but the ties to be here are much stronger than the answer of where to move on to. Either way the transition is uneasy at best. We are stressed, we are stretched, all along we've been taken out of our comfort zone. Our hearts have been fractured, we've lost our hometown, but our hope to rebuild will somehow be found. I'm thankful, I'm grateful, I'm blessed beyond words! Many have come from afar to be here, to guide us, to show us, perhaps to help find us. We're slowly moving on, we're traveling forward, though at times we seem captured by a broken past moment. We've started a plan; we're walking on new land & we're stepping in new ground. This is the time we'll see who we are, what we're made of & how we'll stand. Let us "dare to dream", beyond what we feel. We'll begin to believe & seek once again, for that unexpected hope to call home.

RISING FROM THE ASHES

"*I* didn't know.... was this only a dream?" I thought to myself as I tossed & turned after a sleepless midnight stir. I quickly awoke as I finally realized, I was dreaming of living like nothing had happened or ever occurred. Disheartened, I gathered my purse, cup of joe, turned on some blues & drove down the road. I was hoping to stop all the frustrating questions that kept going round & around in my head. As I slowly drove passed the large iron gates, I took a quick glance at a familiar landmark that looked out of place. I could not believe this, it seemed so amazing, like time had stood still, or maybe just missed it. I gazed at the presence of some remarkable trees, untouched by the fire they escaped that hot blaze. The arms of their branches embraced the blue sky, like the hands of our prayers reaching up toward the heavens. They were valiant, victorious & survived through the flames; they defeated the enemy, "to death not today"! It seemed so ironic, this scene was iconic, in the heart of our city, there was life in our gravestone garden. Our historical cemetery, the potter's field, had battled the fire of those who were buried. Like a bright shining light through the shadow of dark, it was a breath of fresh air, this appearance of life. I wanted to run barefoot, free through the trees, capture the essence, of the tall green pines in the cool gentle breeze. But then all around me I looked & I saw, chaos & ruins that surrounded it all. That hot autumn day I could not erase, it had changed us forever, touched us deeper than ever. I wanted to scream, I was tempted to shout, to yell at this world laying broken & still! So I drove down through town, wiped the tears from my face, when I spotted yellow daffodils springing up all around. Was it Johnny Appleseed who changed the sowers plan? Or maybe the Gold miner's daughter who had a prospectors pan. Whoever, whatever, whenever it happened, it changed my perspective to see beauty for ashes. I turned at the corner, my eyes were surprised, a once barren tree was now covered with lavender blossoms! For an instant, a moment, it seemed like somehow, I'd stepped back in time before the madness began. Just then my questions were finally answered, now I saw clearly to what had just happened. We can't change the past, though that's what we want most, but we can paint today with a vision of hope. A plan to set forth a new life for ourselves, begins with a start to finish the race. Let us strive to be bold, take a chance to be brave, arise like the Phoenix & say, "to death not today"! Never forget who we are, what we've done, we're in this together, we are stronger as one! As God is our witness, let's honor our past, as we are a people who are rising from the ashes!

HOLDING ONTO HOPE

*Y*ou definitely know that you walk alone, when you don't even recognize where you are; can't remember what place was once standing there, or you quickly forget how you got there. Can't find the perfect words to describe how it feels when everything is so different. Nothing seems right & now the new norm is, well quite frankly, whatever is best or however it goes. There's a sweet comfort & a real security embedded in us, when things are consistent & unchanging. Like clockwork, there's a regular routine & like a familiar melody, the song remains the same. We knew the gas station that was at the street light corner near the drug store. It was across the main road from the grocery market, that was right next door to the candy shop. Grandma lived on the other side of town & brothers house was only two streets down, from the little league baseball field. Now we live in an, "under construction" town, that has no landmarks or boundaries. There are more out of town workers than permanent residents & less people & friends than we know. Memorable moments in our short-lived lives, happen at times when we least expect it. Like the joyful news of a new baby arrival, seeing an old friend at a class reunion, the first-time kiss from our sweetheart, or the last goodbye to our precious loved one. Now we have a different kind of history to remember, one which we want to undo but can't; nor can we seem to forget. Our never-ending story looks to only get worse before it begins to get better; as we watch our crumbled world get put back together again. But I want to remember this sojourners journey. What valuable lessons I've learned, that have left a lasting impression on this long dark winding road. I will not take for granted, the comforts of home sweet home ever again, or the companionship of having a close dear friend. The thoughtful gifts of a stranger I'd never met, or the blessed assurance of my loving family, who tenderly held me while I wept. My joy is more heart felt because my sorrow is deeper. My patience is longer because of the disappointment I've had when at my wits end. My love is now stronger in my family circle, my pain is less suffered because of the loyalty & honor of real friends. Out of the Ashes was born from a fire that burned & shattered my own little world. It pierced & touched the heart of my soul. We knew that our lives would be forever changed. Yet through it, we continued to hold onto hope, as we realized things would never be the same. Because of this I dare now say, I am thankful for His hand that heals the hurting heart, His strength that mends the weary soul & His unfailing love that puts the broken pieces of our fragile lives back together again.

THIS IS PARADISE

*L*ooking through my stained-glass window across the darkened landscape, I see the Creator's painted artwork of spring arising. Barren plains of bright green grass softly cover rolling hills & canyon views, like a velvet moss thrown blanket. Multicolored scenes of wildflower blossoms grace the empty fields. Like Mary's quite contrary garden, with silver bells & cockle shells & marigolds all in a row. Rushing rivers fill the many small creek beds, from constant rains & snow packed mountains; creating mini waterfalls, flowing down the rough cliff's edge. Our low tide lake has now reached high, about to reach the border line, where flying geese & boaters share the crisp cool water play. This my friends is Paradise! A fresh bold start has now begun, cleansed the ground & cleared the land; to bear the birth of newfound life that breathes & blooms again. Though blackened trees still stand dark, the season's change has brought some light to gather one a thought. Perhaps a lil spark, of bringing hope & inspiration to our ridge view canyon folk. I know our hearts still break for our broken little town. Yet as we watch this season's change, I hope we shall remember the good times that we had & not just see the ugly, or only see the bad. Like when we danced the night away to Mustang Sally's song, with our very own homegrown bands; at the Annual Blues & Brews or our summer Farmers Market stands! We shared a love for Ridge Strong life; helped peel, core & bake some fresh apple pies from our local Noble Orchard store. Time has come today, this change has now begun, we're moving forward in a new direction to overcome this winter affliction. This is a call to the wild adventurer, a shout to the wounded warrior, a plea to the brave at heart! What once was lost will soon be found, as we are rising up from this broken ground. I know this task is daunting, it's sometimes vastly haunting. But as we choose to walk this rugged path, let's break some bread, say a prayer, offer a plea & wipe the dust from our weary feet. We've stayed the course, gone the distance, been tested, pulled & tried our patience. But through the raging fire, our hearts burn with desire to a call to arms. Open the gates, raise the flag & man the forts! If God be for us, who can be against us! This is not just a place, this is not just our home, this is what we call Paradise!

DOWN BY THE RIVER

*W*anna go down to the river, down to the river to pray. Gonna go down to the river, gotta wash all these blues away! Just like that old blues song, I'm singing those blues away. I'm watching this falling rain washing the ashes & dirt down the way. There's a healing in that cool river water, that's filled by the tears from heaven. It helps to ease the pain & lifts our sorrow's away. It's soothing, refreshing, reviving & life changing! I remember those wonderful carefree times, sitting on the hot boulder rocks, soaking up the warm summer rays & taking a dip at that cool river spot. It was a time to honestly reflect, spiritually connect & quiet the noise in my anxious mind. I was hoping & looking for answers to my numerous questions & life changing directions. My random thoughts & adventurous ways have always taken me to deeper places than most would like to go. I would often venture off the well beaten path & kinda get lost in my own nature walks, or spiritual talks; about life & where I would want to go from here or there. But we're all really searching, always looking, carefully watching, for some kind of obvious sign. Maybe a word of hidden wisdom or just an intuitive gut feeling. Something that will give us some kind of new hope, needed encouragement, or moving inspiration, to know that everything is somehow gonna be alright. But sometimes I'm just so emotionally & mentally exhausted. Like I have been physically running, almost sprinting, in a long-distance race; to try & fix my complicated life & bring some purposeful meaning to this rapid busy pace. It's an uneasy feeling, like something is surely wrong, because nothing really seems quite right. We just want to feel like it's all gonna be okay, that this moment in time will soon pass somehow, somewhere someday. I'm reminded of that old blues song by Louis Armstrong: "Nobody knows the trouble I've seen, nobody knows my sorrow, nobody knows the trouble I've seen, nobody knows but Jesus"! I feel that, it moves me right down to my soul, as I hear his gravelly voice singing his blues away. I've pondered that song, when the troubles overflow into endless & useless unnerving trials on this road. Gotta let it go, all my sorrows, all my woes, lay this burden down, & put this struggle in the ground! Wanna go down to the river, where the living water flows, gonna meet my Sweet Lord there, let Him carry this heavy load. Going down to the river, gotta go on down to pray, down at the river, gonna wash all my blues away!

Oh my heart, my soul does break, each time I drive on these broken roads. I tell myself, "do not despair, this too shall pass, we shall prevail". A time to end, a time to begin, from the old to the new, we enter this season with a reason to hope. I know this is only a means to an end, a phase in this process to setting the next stage. So I try to rise above this sorrow, but I need to be real with myself. Take a breath, say a prayer, feel the pain, let it go, start again. Gotta change my point of view with a different attitude & remember this truth; that life goes on in other places, but life is also what we make it. It's easy to feel lonely & alone in the crowd of unknowns, when family & friends have packed up & gone, taking all that was left. Those who stayed to carry on, like Wayward Sons & Legion Daughters, marching forward like onward soldiers. When this historical news story stopped, the workers came & cleared our burnt lots. They piled up charred logs on rubble plots & downed our crumbled homes. It's hard to drive through our rustic town, with flag twirlers, tree stompers, Deere drivers & more. There are many hardworking women & masked fellows, in bright colored vests of orange, green & yellow. On a new normal day of driving through town, I patiently waited as the road crew directors continued to stop all the anxious moving traffic. I watched all the busy bee action, then made my way around the cone lined lanes & headed on up to visit a newly opened place. I passed you by, I saw your face, don't know your name, but our eyes did meet. Can't say I looked your way before, but saw you shopping in the grocery store. Now we wave, we say hello, we briefly shared our surviving story. A friendly stranger, now a bonded friend, closer neighbors, kindred spirits. A hug, a handshake, a smile hello, has much more meaning now than ever before. When loved ones come to meet & greet, visit home or sit & eat, my heart is elated, my soul is touched, it soothes this sudden break-up. There is a time to grieve, a time to dance, a time to cry, & a time to laugh. Sometimes just listening shows we care, shares the hurt, helps heal each other. Let's take a chance, one by one let's take a hand & stand together. These times my friend... we are a changing!

SCARS OF THE MOUNTAIN

———

*C*oming down the long narrow road, I gaze up at the barren hillside to catch a glimpse of the lost battlefield. It was not that long ago that I had seen the daring young lions, Nala & Simba, heirs from the king of the mountain, gallantly roaming their lush marked territory. I'd often thought how their eerie presence was one I cautiously respected & admired, but only from a distance. Now my wandering eyes seek to find a similar scene, a familiar memory of warm sunny days, catching Brer Rabbit hopping into his safe bunny hole. Alas, I spot his pounding paws over spiny weeds & burnt mistletoe, as he gathers berries for his midnight dreams. The dried out burned up trees & scorched scarred ground, cries out in vain. I stare at what little remains of once green rolling hills, with plentiful rows of daffodils, lilies, dandelions & fern. This mountain has sadly suffered. It's deeply scarred with the remnants of what so little is left, after so much had been taken in a matter of only a few hours. I feel it's pain, I know it's ache. I share its battle scars from riding the tails of the roar of the beast, that stole the land of the free & the homes of the brave. But as I look upon this harsh terrain, I am moved to the core as I begin to see more of the fresh beginnings of healing. New growth in the grazing land, tiny colorful buds arising from the depth of the charred earth. I confidently smile as I realize that promise I held onto, when I walked through the valley of darkness & came out of the ashes of despair. "He gives us beauty for ashes, joy for mourning & the garment of praise for the spirit of heaviness". I can see His beauty in this handiwork of new life returning through the ashes. The native wildlife & families of flying creatures are slowly returning & giving birth to their innocent offspring young. Healing has begun on the scars of the mountain. We are connected as one, together in this journey, this pilgrimage. My spirit is renewed as the scars from my heart shed the tears of the wounded. Little by little, that underlying joy is released when I see these new beginnings painted across the mountain tops & valley floors. I can give praise for this newness & gift of bringing life to this still beautiful ridge. "Those who plant in tears will harvest with shouts of joy. They weep as they go to plant their seed, but they sing as they return with the harvest".

Psalm 126:5,6

A BEAUTIFUL MESS

---

*O*h, what a beautiful mess! I cannot possibly fill this blank & empty page with enough heartfelt gratitude. I give praise & thanksgiving to God, for all that He has done! What reckless doubt & unspoken thoughts I had, when all was so quickly gone. Though untouched by the fire that surrounded us, we felt so deeply torn. We stared at what it left of our home, not only a terrible mess, but also a scar on our hearts. Like a wandering sojourner, I was looking for a meaningful purpose to this chaos. A reasonable way to find peace & rest. I battled the heat of the loss & the flames that consumed my thoughts. Yet, I found refuge in the old rugged cross! My heart was complete, though broken & shattered, my mind was renewed, though thoughtlessly scattered. My soul was reborn when I felt helpless & useless, as I depended on Him, He held me together. This was my beautiful mess! A delicate balance to the steps of a dance, through the summer seasons & winter songs. I was captured by the One who held the whole world, my little world, in the palm of His hands. I'm no longer alone in the shadow of darkness, walking through the ashes of grief. He tenderly carried me through it, like the footprints in the sand. I am free from harm, safe in His loving arms. Now I'm walking onward, like a conqueror on a quest to make peace with my past. I move forward, one day, one step at a time. We've seen what seemed like an impossible dream, become something more beautiful than before! All in His perfect time. He takes the mess that we are & He uses it, to make something more beautiful in us. Now we are the ones who are blessed, all from this beautiful mess! Oh, what a Savior we have! He gives Beauty for Ashes again & again... my beautiful mess I am.

ALL ITS NAME IMPLIES

I can only imagine what this will be like! In a quiet daydream state of mind, I try to focus on what Paradise could possibly be. As I catch myself from spinning around in an endless circle of meaningless thoughts, I try to envision a better outcome through these many losses. It's hard to see the distant future when we are staring at a torn down town. Paradise. It's challenging at best, for it to be all it's name implies. Our sweet memories are remembered like the light of day. Yet, our bitter losses can capture our thoughts & weaken our weary souls. As I walk on this imperfect path, I'm often faced with looking back in time to face my fears. I must conquer the enemy of defeat, from robbing my joy & stealing the peace, that keeps my feet from slipping again. I remember how the rage of the fire took all we had. Our memorable souvenirs of yesterday's years gone by, like echoes in our minds. We watched the flames take our home, all our hard-earned work, creative projects & a lifetime burned to the ground. The wounds of the battle left scars that grew deep & slowly stole pieces of our hearts, one by one. It was only by careful reflection & prayerful searching, that I was able to find healing, to mend & repair the damage of this heated past. Now I can only imagine what life was like before my own little world crumbled into a pile of metal & ash. But when you really think about it, we always have losses in one form or another. This is how we use loss to make us stronger, build us better & create in us something more beautiful than before. We are over-comers, who rise to the occasion of becoming all that we are created to be! We may be pressed on every side by troubles, but we are not crushed! We may be perplexed, but we will not be driven to despair! We may get knocked down, but we will not be destroyed! Though the enemy like a lion seeks to devour us, we are NEVER abandoned by God! When I see the countless possibilities, I can envision something better than before. We may seem to be at a disadvantage, even severely disabled, but through these losses we are neither. We are just differently abled! It starts with the face in the mirror. We choose a life that rises above the ashes & believing that with God's help, we can make something impossible become possible again! May we again, find Paradise to be all its name implies!

A WALK THRU THE ASHES

This walk is hard, the journey long. It feels like I am dragging my tired feet through the muddy trenches. It's as if I'm carrying a heavy load wherever I go, however I run, or whatever I do. Yet I cannot escape what I must go through. For though this rugged road is hard, I must press on & battle through what has begun. So many have traveled to distant places, with new horizons & different faces. It's still a tremendous hardship, to grieve this terrible loss. Whether near or far, we all are affected by this conflicting lot. Sometimes the weight of our small little world can feel like an anchor, or a chain to our past. We barely can gather a quiet composure, or find some peaceful solace, in this confusing maze & foggy haze of stress filled days. The unending questions that bounce in our heads, have no easy answers or simple suggestions. The multiple choices that add to our list, are too many decisions to make or to fix. Want to scream but no time, need to cry but no tears, have to work but can't move, just don't know what to do! Gotta stop, take a breath, let it go, calm the soul. Say a prayer & believe, we will overcome this, as God brings us through it. What we have endured on this long-broken road, hasn't been easy or light. When it didn't break us, it carefully made us much stronger than we were before. On this stride we have wandered, roamed & trekked, as our faith has been tested, tried & questioned. The times we feel weary & weak, we are held by the One who is near the broken hearted. A towering refuge in the storm, a light in the darkness & a shield to the helpless. Through this journey & path we may fear the unknown, but we're never alone, as God walks beside us & renews & refines us. As we walk thru these ashes, let us trust in the Lord. Now we shall rise up with wings like an eagle & soar past the path, that brought beauty through these ashes!

RENEWED HOPE

How do you mend a broken heart? The songwriter sings, the poet writes & the orator asks. Our losses are many, for some few, maybe extensive or only minor. From our homes to our hearts, with our friends to our loved ones. We all know how little or huge, is the cross that we bear. No matter how hard we try, our hearts cannot heal our open wounds, those deep battle scars or the emotional heartaches. I've tried & failed, time & time again. I can't change myself, I'm unable to fix others or stop the ones that I love from hurting themselves. Where do I go to lighten this grip that tightens & weighs on my soul? Here I sit, unable to move through the weight of ache & tears of sorrow. Self pity, maybe. Heavy load, yes. Deep thoughts, of course. Reflection, intervention, perception, destruction. All intertwine in my head, bouncing around & confusing my mind. I'm thinking, maybe dreaming or feeling too much. Yet I cannot let go though I know that I must! Close my eyes, say a prayer, quiet the noise of my thoughts. Finally I feel the soft gentle touch of His loving hand. This is more than just something of calming myself or trying to settle my tense edgy nerves. There's a peaceful rest, a silent comfort & a sweet tender moment, as I realize this truth. It's not up to me. Only this choice to give in is on me, not to give up but to sincerely choose Him. From the words of the Psalmist, my questions are answered. My doubt in myself although honestly real, is replaced & restored with a trust & belief in the Lord. Through this hope, I'm renewed, I'm fallen for His love. Now He is able to heal & to mend, my brokenness, my heart & my weary soul. "Unless the Lord had helped me, I would soon have settled in the silence of the grave. I cried out, "I am slipping!" but Your unfailing love, O Lord, supported me. When doubts filled my mind, Your comfort gave me renewed hope & cheer".

Psalm 94:17-19

89

PARADISE STRONG

"*For* when I am weak, then I am strong." The writer speaks with conviction, of knowing where his strength & endurance comes from. It's not difficult to see this same tenacity in the hearts of our towns people, our youth & the elderly homesteaders who have strongly made their claim. I'm impressed with the comrade spirit that embraces this community. It's like the protective bobcats that mark their territory & take their stand to defend their own. This beautiful & mystical animal has an intriguing & historic life on the Ridge. Their story is one that gives us a wonderful comparative illustration of the strength that comes through weakness. As through their desperate threats of extinction, the bobcat continued to prove that their livelihood was one of resilience; much like the steadfastness of our very own town. Consider the brave hunters they are, since the bobcat is much smaller in stature than most felines. Yet they are able to take down much larger prey during the leanest times of scarcity & starvation. It's no wonder that the perfect mascot for our High School has been the mighty Bobcat. It represents our undefeated team spirit! This same oneness, determined motivation & warrior attitude, can be seen through the gallant efforts of so many. We are only a few, but we're courageous & brave. Our adversities are great, but we're vigilant & unafraid. Alone we may be, but together we're one. Although we're weak, we can become strong! The writer's words speak bold & true; "Not that I was ever in need, for I have learned how to be content with whatever I have. I know how to live on almost nothing, or with everything. I have learned the secret of living in every situation, whether it is with a full stomach or empty, with plenty or little. For I can do everything through Christ, who gives me strength". Through these difficult times, we've shared our hearts, homes & our lives with each other, as the caring community we are. We've learned to find the strength when we had nothing left to give. As the trail leads the Bobcat to return to its habitat, so the strength of Paradise shall continue to live!

Philippians 4:11-13

PRECIOUS SEED

"For everything there is a season... a time to plant & a time to harvest." Wise words to embrace as we continue to take great strides to move forward & rebuild our lives. We've often heard the saying, "grow where you're planted". Hard to do when we've been uprooted from our home sweet home. Yet I've often found comfort & healing in the green thumb gardening of sowing new seed. The replanting & repotting brings joy to my heart when I see the wonderful growth of those beautiful blooms. It's so rewarding to see the work of our hands, after breaking up the hard ground & tilling the land. The fruit bearing trees & green leafed stalks, are a sight to behold for anyone's home! Although this is often more joyous than tedious, there're moments when the work is a difficult effort to endure. I've worked the soil with my weary hands, as I buried my sorrow & hoped for a better tomorrow. I've watered the new sprouts with my weeping tears & prayed for the strength to see the beauty through the ashes. There's a reason for this season. It's a time to diligently work to replant what's been lost & restore what hasn't been forgotten. As we continue to slowly heal, let's plant that seed which gives birth to new hope. Let's tenderly nourish & feed this, as we lovingly water & care for it. So attentive we'll be to protect it, as we watch it take root through the path of resistance. Then we'll see that amazing growth that we'd never had known, if we'd never had sown, that precious seed. It's such a splendid reflection of what we become! It's when we finally let go & release our scattered dreams, broken hearts & deepest desires to the Lord. We place our seeds of sorrow, gifts & talents in the ground, laying it all down to the One who is faithful to gently heal, delicately mend & tenderly make us. "I have seen the burden God has placed on us all. Yet God has made everything beautiful for its own time. He has planted eternity in the human heart..." our precious seed.

Ecc. 3:1,2,10

DREAM CATCHER

*O*ne day, one step, one moment at a time. This is our life. Trying to see what's ahead instead of behind, is a constant challenge. There are no strategic plans or written directions to make our unspoken dreams become a new reality. Yet we cannot see, if we don't believe. Our faith is the substance that sustains & helps us to regain the courage to see the impossible. If we question our motives with scattered thoughts of fear & doubt, then we shall fail! Mistakes, I've made a few. Made the wrong decision, probably more often than I want to remember. But, we all have, we're human! Yet the errors, bad judgement & crazy times we've had, can be used to our advantage if we learn from them. There are always tragic losses, difficult hardships & futile struggles. It's how we grow stronger while we walk this weary road & imperfect path. I don't understand it. I definitely don't like this. But I do know, that is how we build character, strength & resilience. That's how dreams are made; from the fruit of our life. What we choose to recreate & rebuild through the scars of the battlefields, will give us the ability to rekindle this hope & restore our dreams. At the end of the day, we know we will see, the setting sunset against the painted blue sky. Just as sure as the day is done, the light of the moon shall rise & the dark of night will begin. It's all so beautiful, the Creators hand, no mistakes, His perfect plan. We're all a part of this wonderful life, created by His love; our Maker's dream. I want to catch the vision & rise to the moment of becoming another.... Dream Catcher!

"Do not rejoice over me [amid my tragedies], O my enemy! Though I fall, I will rise; Though I sit in the darkness [of distress], the LORD is a light for me."

MICAH 7:8

THIS IS OUR STORY

---

*R*emembering the past, those quaint precious moments...

Alone with my sweetheart on a short summer drive, singing to the radio, we felt so alive! Riding down the streets in that ole' classic car, while the wind in my hair filled the crisp night air. Sipping a glass of cool lemonade, we sat in the shade of our tall Oak trees. It was fresh, so inviting & excitingly new, as we danced through the times & the days of our lives. Strutting a step like we knew what to do, but our heart was just beating to the sound of a tune! It was our love-song, bedside story & night serenades. But little did we know, we were creating something special, we were making our home. I can't forget or casually erase, a whole lifetime of memories, moments & events. Though this struggle to remember when the losses are much, the times that we shared & the things that we'd lost. Can't drive down that road like before or escape from the heat, beneath our leafy green trees. It won't be the same for everything has changed. Our homes & town have been shattered & torn. Our hearts & lives have been broken & worn. I want to be stronger & braver, as we move into the next chapter of a different new role. I'm taking a breath & turning the page, trusting God to rewrite this journey's next stage. One word, one line, one step at a time, today is the first day of the rest of our lives. Now, we begin again... this is our story.

"Wait patiently for the Lord. Be brave and courageous.
Yes, wait patiently for the Lord."

Psalms 27:14 NLT

TADPOLES, WATERMELONS & SUNFLOWER

*O*ut of the unexpected comes something amazing! Isn't that how things often happen? We may never know the outcome of how our life will be... until the unexplained, unbelievable is right before our eyes! Who can beautifully create or mysteriously perform, such wondrous feats of amazement.... all for us to see? Just gaze upon the painted rainbow across the cloudy sky, after listening to the cracklings of a lightning thunderstorm. I've seen that kind of beauty, arise above the dark, as I've walked across the rocky path & held on by a thread. Our world, our lives are always changing. Yet it's easy not to recognize or appreciate the simple blessings. Until one day, it happens. Finally, I see it. Something quite unusual... tiny tadpoles, watermelons & one bright yellow sunflower. They all appeared somehow, underneath my garden thumb, without me ever tending or planting any one! Overnight without a clue, I barely saw them move & then I had a tadpole farm, until they slowly grew. Another day I noticed, a wild looking weed. It blossomed from a stray seed & gave me watermelons! Then I saw that lonesome sunflower. So majestic was it's bloom, as it briefly stood its ground. It kissed my world & greeted me, before the sun dried up it's leaves. I'd watered, watched & waited, while all three began to grow, amazed at how this blessing, taught me more than I could know. Those black-eyed seeds from my flower of faith, gave me precious newfound hope. Replant, restore what had been lost in the time before the storm. That fruitful melon brought a sweetness, to tenderly remind me. He can heal the brokenness of the hard & bitter past. How fast life changes, as I'd watched my tadpoles, yet they barely seemed to grow. Those slinky legs & arms, replaced their floppy tails & one by one they quickly bailed the pail! Now I see how life reshapes me, as I try to become, the best at what I'll be. These simplest things I've learned from the humor of this story; tadpoles, watermelons.... & one beautiful sunflower.

"Unfailing love and truth have met together. Righteousness and peace have kissed! Truth springs up from the earth, and righteousness smiles down from heaven. Yes, the Lord pours down his blessings."

Psalm 85:10-12 NLT

STEPPING STONES

*W*e all wondered when we were younger. "What will we be?"... when we grow up & get older. Then here we are, already there... living the Dream! Perhaps it's not exactly, how we quietly imagined or perfectly envisioned. Maybe you took a little detour off the map, only to find yourself having to backtrack. I often thought that my passions & dreams would happen someday, somewhere, someway. But, life always changes & time never stands still. It's always passing. Tick tock, round the clock we go, where it stops nobody knows! Before we know it, yesterday's gone, today is here & tomorrow will come. It plays no favoritism to life or pays any respect for age. Sometimes I have to stop myself, forgive my disappointments, accept a new vision & remember the good that has come along the way. All that is lovely & true, beautiful & amazing, precious & real. These are more important to focus & ponder on. It's not hard to see the bad times & ugly events of the past. But it's better to seek for the truth, see the blessings & know that sweet peace that passes all understanding. We have to be willing to roll with the punches & let the chip on our shoulder roll down off the sweat of our back. I'm learning to be okay with that; willing to give up what I've got to let go. Because these are the days that are making it count; my choices, this moment, our time & these steps. I'm not just tumbling along down the road, as the song, "Like a Rolling Stone" sings. But I'm changing the tune, making a home in my heart, wherever I go. Unlike the verses, that speaks of a meaningless purpose, I need to have some meaningful direction & soulful connections. I might feel like the songwriter speaks of being on my own, but I know I am never alone or even a complete unknown. So I'm building a bridge across all the deep losses & making a path from these hard stepping stones. Like the Potter forms the clay of the earth to the wheel, He is able to make something more beautiful from this! Shake the dust from the man, shape a life with a plan, I am like a rolling stone; but I am created & held in the palm of His hands.

BRAVE HEARTS

She's looking out the window, standing... with a sharpened sword in hand. Nothing much is left in the midst of all the chaos. Out of the smoke He arises, she catches a glimpse of Him. His arms are carrying some & He's holding up the others. The weary, weak & tired, who've crossed this rugged road in this battlefield called, "Home". She sees these brave, courageous ones who've fought this trying battle; survivors of the fearless, who've stood the test of time. The tears, the pain, the sorrow, like a war that never ends. But victims of a tragedy, a loss or broken heart, is never just a quick fix or an easy fight to win. She cannot lead their destined path nor step into their shattered dreams of midnight strolls down darkened roads. They've traveled on those lonesome trails of wandering thoughts & deep regrets of disappointments of the past. Now she stands, her hand tightly grips the strength of a cold steel blade. It keeps all safe within her care as she secretly walks beside them & quietly defends. It was cut & made by the heat of a flame & shaped by the Masters hand. It breaks the cords that bind the hearts to release the pain & calm the storm. She stares in the distance, the shadows lurk in the still of the night on this moonlight watch. She sees the ones that bear the test of being pressed on every side, but they're not crushed beneath the weight. Though perplexed in trials, they're not left in deep despair because never are they abandoned by God. These are the ones who are held by the Lord of Heavens Armies. She is that one, their Guardian Angel, who stands in the gap to guard these precious ones she calls... Brave Hearts.

ACKNOWLEDGEMENTS

To my husband Jim, thank you for your loving support & always believing in me; together we found beauty through the ashes. To Susan Fisher, my dear friend who graciously edited each entry, your friendship & love is such a blessing to me, thank you. To my talented son Jim G Peppler, you continue to amaze me, thank you for sharing your incredible & inspiring art. Jesse K Peppler, your photo has touched so many lives, thank you for catching the perfect moment on a special day. Thank you Alicia Turner, for capturing such an awesome photo. Cindy Lee Hoover, thank you so much for giving your time to this project, your wonderful photography is breathtaking, you are truly amazing! Thank you Jessie Groeschen for your magnificent Bobcat carving! Elena Cioluca, thank you for sharing your glorious Guardian Angel, truly a memorable work of beauty! Shane Grammer you have inspired many to look beyond the ashes of despair & hope for a better tomorrow, thank you for all your beautiful Murals. Nicole Franco, I couldn't have done this book without you, I am so grateful for your help. Above all, I am eternally thankful to God. Without His love, inspiration & encouragement, none of this would have been possible.

PHOTO AND ARTWORK INDEX

Antoinette Peppler is an artist at heart. She's always loved writing poetry, journaling and songwriting. Her love for God is expressed in her inspirational stories and devotion to family, music and nature.

As part of a military family, Antoinette has traveled extensively throughout the United States and overseas. After High School, she went to audio engineering school in LA, where she learned to record with top engineers in the music industry and has recorded in-studio and live concert settings. Antoinette followed in her mom's footsteps carrying on a family tradition—training in the culinary arts and even becoming a professional cake decorator. She continues to use these skills to this day. Later, she started a home called The Sisters' House for young women to live and share their faith. Antoinette also worked with an evangelical outreach program to minister to homeless orphans in Mexico.

At Bible College, she met the love of her life. Together they settled in Paradise California, where they raised a family, led worship and played music with various groups over the years. The beautiful home her husband and three sons built in the hills of Paradise made national news when it was completely destroyed in the 2016 Saddle Fire. They've since rebuilt a new home and then the historic 2018 Camp Fire spared their residence but tragically, devastated their hometown and entire ridge community. This is her story of coming "Out of the Ashes," sharing her journey of hope and encouragement to help those who are on the same path.

LinkBook

linkbooklegacies.com